But I Waited and Waited

H.C. McCrae

Trilogy Christian Publishers
A Wholly Owned Subsidiary of Trinity Broadcasting Network
2442 Michelle Drive
Tustin, CA 92780

Copyright © 2023 by Helen C. McCrae

All rights reserved, including the right to reproduce this book or portions thereof in any form whatsoever.

Cover design by: Cornerstone Creative Solutions

For information, address Trilogy Christian Publishing
Rights Department, 2442 Michelle Drive, Tustin, Ca 92780.
Trilogy Christian Publishing/ TBN and colophon are trademarks of Trinity Broadcasting Network.

For information about special discounts for bulk purchases, please contact Trilogy Christian Publishing.

Manufactured in the United States of America

Trilogy Disclaimer: The views and content expressed in this book are those of the author and may not necessarily reflect the views and doctrine of Trilogy Christian Publishing or the Trinity Broadcasting Network.

10 9 8 7 6 5 4 3 2 1

Library of Congress Cataloging-in-Publication Data is available.

ISBN 978-1-68556-026-3 (Print Book)
ISBN 978-1-68556-027-0 (ebook)

Dedication

To my brother and guardian angel, Carlos. I miss you so much! You were so excited when I told you over three years ago about, *But I Waited and Waited*. You told me to trust God in all His ways, to be obedient, and to allow the Lord to use me regardless of the tasks. Carlos, I was obedient. Thank you for the talks, the prayers, the encouragement, and the love that you have always shown me and everyone around you.

Thank you for showing me what the highest reward of waiting truly looks like. You led with strength and taught with love. This book is proof, that although you are in heaven, your prayers are still being answered and always will. This is for you!

With love,

Your Sister

Acknowledgements

Lord, thank You for choosing me for this assignment!

Dad, thank you that giving up was never an option. Thank you for your love and all you've done. I love and appreaciate you so much!

Mom, my heavenly angel, thank you for your love and covering our family with your prayers.

To my children, because of all of you, I truly know how to love and be patient. I love you all very much!

To my husband, thank you for believing in the story of CeCe. Thank you for being there every step of the way during this process. I love you dearly!

To my siblings, thank you for your love, encouragement, and being so excited about this journey! It means everything to me!

To the Ward's, Sheila, and the Lowther's, I am so grateful for your timing in my life. Thank you and I love you all!

To the Thomas Family, thank you for the love and foundation that could never leave me, but constantly leads me.

Ms. Juliana Wilson, thank you for giving me the opportunity to begin my journey in Japan with shaping little minds.

Pastor Jeff and Pastor Kim Little, thank you for your leadership and guidance.

To every single child that I had the honor of teaching, because of you, I found an integral part of my purpose. Thank you!

To the Terri Lynne Lokoff Foundation and the United States Air Force, thank you for understanding and acknowledging my love for impacting children from around the world.

Foreword

The author writes about an impatient little girl name CeCe, who learns the value of waiting. The author has written the story in a simple form that allows children to understand what patience means and the benefits of patiently waiting. The concept of the book is a gift and a lesson that can be valued by people of all ages and cultural backgrounds.

Introduction

The desires of children are great, but their impatience, is often greater. I believe that it is important for children to understand the value and benefits of patiently waiting. If this can be understood at a young age, I could only image how beneficial this will be as they transition to young adulthood, then to adulthood.

I can remember being anxious as a child, and hearing adults say, "Wait, just wait" on things of various natures. Most of the time, there was never an explanation about why waiting was necessary. Usually, "Wait just wait" was followed by, "Because I said so." I believe that many people can relate to hearings that one time or another.

As you will see, CeCe is quite impatient, but learns a valuable lesson in listening to the guidance of her mother and waiting.

I've found that even in my own experiences, that not waiting and being patient has caused me to have to wait even longer for the things that were meant for me. The same thing applies to CeCe. She realizes that her mind could have never fathomed how great of a treat, was in store for her if she patiently waited.

In the end, CeCe realizes that she should have waited and waited.

But I Waited and Waited

CeCe ran in the kitchen when she saw her mommy and said, "Mommy—, I thought that you left to go to the store already."

"You haven't given me a chance to get my car keys. Oh CeCe! You're so antsy," Mommy said.

"But I am not tiny. I do not crawl on the ground. I do not live in the dirt, and I don't BITE, Mommy! I'm not an insect."

"Oh CeCe! Did you think that I was saying that you were an ant?" Mommy giggled.

"But you said that I was being antsy," said CeCe.

"When I say that you are being antsy, it means that you're not being patient," Mommy said.

"Patient? Who's Patient? I'm CeCe. My name is CeCe. Why did you call me Patient?"

Her mommy giggled once again and said, "My sweet SWEET, CeCe. I wasn't calling you the name Patient."

Maybe I should have named her Patience, she thought.

Before her mother could finish explaining what she meant, CeCe asked her, "Well, why did you say that I wasn't being patient?"

"When you want something, you never want to wait. While you are waiting on something that you want, you can be do something else so that you won't think about what you're waiting on," mommy replied.

CeCe said, "Ummm okay. I'll try to be…ummm. What's that word again?" she asked.

"Patient," mommy said.

CeCe replied, "Okay, so when are you going to the grocery store?"

Her mom looked at her with annoyance and said, "CeCe, I'm getting ready to go right now and I want you to stay here with your brother, Kevin. I will be back shortly, so no snacks until I get back. I will bring you a treat when I return."

"Kevin!" mommy called. Kevin came downstairs and calmly said, "Yes?"

"I'm going to the store. I need you to watch your little sister until I get back," she said.

Thirty minutes went by and CeCe could no longer wait.

"Kevin, can you give me the biggest and the bestest treat we got?" she asked.

Not knowing that mommy told CeCe not to have any treats while she was gone, Kevin said "Do you mean that you would like the biggest and the best treat that we have?"

CeCe said "Yeah, yeah!" in excitement. Kevin gave her a small cup of ice cream. Though CeCe wasn't too thrilled about the treat, she settled for it anyway.

As soon as CeCe was finished with her ice cream, she could hear her mommy pulling into the garage.

When her mom came into the house she said, "CeCe, I'm back and I have a special treat for you."

With joy and excitement, CeCe jumped up and down saying, "What is it?! What is it?!"

"It's your absolute favorite treat in the whole world."

CeCe yelled, "A strawberry cupcake?!"

Her mom said, "Not just any strawberry cupcake, but the biggest and the best strawberry cupcake I could buy with tons of sprinkles in and on it." CeCe never had a treat quite like that one.

Mommy noticed a sticky mess on CeCe's face and asked, "CeCe, did you have a treat while I was gone?" CeCe put her head down and answered, "Yes."

Mommy was very disappointed. "Because you didn't wait on me to bring your treat, now you're going to have to wait another day to have it," she said.

"When we are patient and wait, we usually receive bigger and better things than we can ever imagine. That is one of the awesome things about waiting, CeCe."

"You are right mommy. I didn't know that you were going to bring me such a gigantic treat back," CeCe said.

With sheer sadness, CeCe said, "BUT I should have waited and waited…"

CPSIA information can be obtained
at www.ICGtesting.com
Printed in the USA
BVHW011936200223
658864BV00001B/1